T0255782

C++/CLI PRIMER

FOR .NET DEVELOPMENT

Vivek Ragunathan

Apress®

C++/CLI Primer: For .NET Development

Vivek Ragunathan
San Jose, USA

ISBN-13 (pbk): 978-1-4842-2366-6   ISBN-13 (electronic): 978-1-4842-2367-3
DOI 10.1007/978-1-4842-2367-3

Library of Congress Control Number: 2016959666

Managing Director: Welmoed Spahr
Lead Editor: Steve Anglin
Technical Reviewer: Rohan Walia
Editorial Board: Steve Anglin, Pramila Balan, Laura Berendson, Aaron Black,
    Louise Corrigan, Jonathan Gennick, Robert Hutchinson, Celestin Suresh John,
    Nikhil Karkal, James Markham, Susan McDermott, Matthew Moodie,
    Natalie Pao, Gwenan Spearing
Coordinating Editor: Mark Powers
Copy Editor: Deanna Hegle
Compositor: SPi Global
Indexer: SPi Global
Artist: SPi Global

Distributed to the book trade worldwide by Springer Science+Business Media New York, 233 Spring Street, 6th Floor, New York, NY 10013. Phone 1-800-SPRINGER, fax (201) 348-4505, e-mail orders-ny@springer-sbm.com, or visit www.springeronline.com. Apress Media, LLC is a California LLC and the sole member (owner) is Springer Science + Business Media Finance Inc (SSBM Finance Inc). SSBM Finance Inc is a **Delaware** corporation.

For information on translations, please e-mail rights@apress.com, or visit www.apress.com.

Apress and friends of ED books may be purchased in bulk for academic, corporate, or promotional use. eBook versions and licenses are also available for most titles. For more information, reference our Special Bulk Sales–eBook Licensing web page at www.apress.com/bulk-sales.

Any source code or other supplementary materials referenced by the author in this text are available to readers at www.apress.com/9781484223666. For detailed information about how to locate your book's source code, go to www.apress.com/source-code/. Readers can also access source code at SpringerLink in the Supplementary Material section for each chapter.

Printed on acid-free paper

To my wife, Neelima.

Contents

About the Author

Vivek Ragunathan is a technology architect with extensive experience in architecting, re-architecting, designing, and implementing large-scale back-end/web applications. He calls himself language agnostic, polyglot, linguist, and linguaphile. He loves playing with different programming languages and is particularly interested in experimenting in how a language yields itself in solving a given problem succinctly and elegantly. He is skillful in object-oriented design, programming, and methodologies and thoughtfully borrows and applies functional programming concepts. Apart from programming, he loves writing, photography (digital but not manipulated).

Vivek writes about programming on his blog **A Developer's Experience** (http://vivekragunathan.wordpress.com).

About the Technical Reviewer

Rohan Walia is a senior software consultant with extensive experience in client/server, web-based, and enterprise application development. He is an Oracle Certified ADF (Application Development Framework) Implementation Specialist and a Sun Certified Java Programmer. Rohan is responsible for designing and developing end-to-end applications consisting of various cutting-edge frameworks and utilities. His areas of expertise are Oracle ADF, Oracle WebCenter, Fusion, Spring, Hibernate, and Java/J2EE. When he's not working, Rohan loves to play tennis, hike, and travel. Rohan would like to thank his wife, Deepika Walia, for using all her experience and expertise when reviewing this book.

About the Technical Reviewer

Introduction

C++/CLI is unattractive, clumsy, and hard when compared to other modern programming languages that run on the .NET platform. That's because it is powerful. Like light that can be viewed as a wave or particle, C++/CLI can be exercised as an unmanaged or managed language or actually as a sandwich language to do mixed-mode programming, which is its real power. That's also why it is unique.

In this book, I present some of the important aspects of the C++/ CLI language that usually pose a barrier to programmers new to the language. I believe that this book will guide you through that barrier. Beyond that barrier lies a world of hard-core programming on the .NET platform.

This book is not an extensive guide to master the C++\CLI programming language; rather, it is quick start learning material that offers an easier way for an unmanaged C++ programmer to enter the world of managed programming, still sticking to C++. The book should be helpful also for a C#, or VB.NET, or a pure managed programmer too to program in C++\CLI where the two programming worlds merge to offer the most powerful programming environment.

© Vivek Ragunathan 2016

V. Ragunathan, *C++/CLI Primer*, DOI 10.1007/978-1-4842-2367-3_1

In the book, I focus on highlighting features that distinguish C++/CLI from C++ and other managed languages in general. In that regard, I aim this book at programmers who have reasonable experience programming in C++ or one of the other unmanaged languages. This book is not appropriate for people beginning to program; nor is C++/CLI, for that matter.

I hope what you learn from this book proves to be useful in your everyday programming life.

Comparisons of C++\CLI with C# or other .NET languages have not been made often, but if they are made, they are not to win arguments but to show the differences and to understand and appreciate gotchas and subtleties. There are absolutely no references in this book to the **obsolete** Managed Extensions for C++.

So let's jump right in!!!

Words of Agreement

The word **unmanaged** in the broader sense encompasses any and all technologies (Win32, COM, …) and programming languages (C++, VB, Pascal, …) prior to the inception of .NET. The word **managed** refers to the .NET technology itself and only those programming languages that support programming on the .NET platform. The words **object** and **instance** have been used interchangeably for the managed object.

The .NET refers to or is the programming technology, platform, and standard. CLR (Common Language Runtime) is the implementation of .NET and is the runtime engine (platform) that programming languages such as C++/CLI or C# generate IL (intermediate language) code to get hosted against. CLR is the virtual processor that executes the IL generated by the various programming languages available for programming on the .NET platform. C++\CLI is the superior one of them. In this book, in its entirety, I attempt to help you start learning the same.

© Vivek Ragunathan 2016
V. Ragunathan, *C++/CLI Primer*, DOI 10.1007/978-1-4842-2367-3_2

In the rest of the book, C++ means the ANSI (American National Standards Institute) ISO (International Organization for Standardization; ANSI-ISO) C++ (originally conceived by Bjarne Stroustrup). It is for programming in the unmanaged world and cannot be used for programming on the .NET platform. C++\CLI is not the same, and in this book, I will delve into that in more detail. It must be considered as an entirely different language whose subset is the features and facilities of the ANSI-ISO C++. For the content of this article, unmanaged refers to programming through C++, although generally speaking, it is equivalent to programming with any of the other unmanaged programming languages such as VB (Visual Basic).

Unmanaged Programming Brief

We have to reap what we sow. I mean, in C++ (unmanaged world), if you allocate memory by new/malloc, then it is your responsibility to deallocate memory using delete/free. Forgetting to deallocate the allocated memory after the formal consumption results in memory leaks. The compiler is tightly bound to the underlying operating system (OS) and/or hardware and uses the APIs (Application Program Interfaces) exposed by the underlying OS for programming.

© Vivek Ragunathan 2016
V. Ragunathan, *C++/CLI Primer*, DOI 10.1007/978-1-4842-2367-3_3

Managed Programming Brief

Programming in the managed world comprises the programming language used, the libraries (called the **B**ase **C**lass **L**ibrary [BCL]), and the CLR itself. The BCL is the gateway to the platform on which the program will be executed. The BCL provides all the APIs for programming and is organized under various namespaces corresponding to the service intended— file system, memory, network, user interface, process and threads, and so forth. One of the several facilities in managed programming is automatic memory management—allocation is our wish, deallocation is automatically taken care of by the CLR by a process called "Garbage Collection."

© Vivek Ragunathan 2016
V. Ragunathan, *C++/CLI Primer*, DOI 10.1007/978-1-4842-2367-3_4

Types in the managed world are entities that bear information and on which operations are carried by calling methods. Each type is unique by itself. For using the types, we create instances of types and work with it. Types (and their associated operations) are packaged and deployed as assemblies. An "assembly" is the ultimate unit of deployment, and is the building block of a CLR-based application. An assembly is versioned, which serves as its identity. An assembly is similar to the dynamic link library for the unmanaged world, although assemblies are themselves dynamic link libraries or executables. Types packaged in an assembly are accessible from outside based on the accessibility marked for the type. For instance, a class type marked `public` is accessible from outside and so are its methods that are marked `public`.

What Is C++\CLI?

I know that might sound like a boring start. But C++\CLI needs a formal introduction. ANSI/ISO C++ is one of the mainstream programming languages for programming on Windows. The .NET is a new platform/technology that offers hardware/platform independence unlike other older technologies. It has its own execution engine: a virtual processor, which is the CLR. While C++ generates an executable for the target platform, the managed programming languages generate IL code for the CLR. Programming languages are required to be compliant with CLI and the CTS (Common Type System) to be used for programming in the managed world.

© Vivek Ragunathan 2016
V. Ragunathan, *C++/CLI Primer*, DOI 10.1007/978-1-4842-2367-3_5

ANSI/ISO C++ cannot be used to program on the .NET platform because it is not compliant with the CLI/CTS. Hence, C++\CLI is a new language (like C++ for C) that was invented to program on the .NET platform. Though the syntax, grammar, and some of the rules are the same as C++, it must not be considered just an extension over C++. Instead, C++ is a subset of C++\CLI, which is not the ultimate intent of the invention.

C++\CLI is a secular programming language, which means it can be used for managed or unmanaged or mixed-mode programming. Hence, legacy code that cannot be ported to the .NET platform (using C# or any other .NET language of choice) in a short time span can be easily ported with C++\CLI. Also, any new code in such legacy C++ projects can be written as pure managed code. It also bridges the gap for the pure managed languages that are otherwise handicapped in using unmanaged code. So, your C# project can now use your complex algorithms or the bunch of hi-fi utilities written in ANSI C++, just with a C++\CLI wrapper over them.

Types and Object Creation

There are three data types in C++\CLI—reference, value, and native.

Native types are those that already exist with C++, say `int`, `float`, `class`, `struct`, and so forth. An instance of these types is allocated on the stack when created statically. When created dynamically (using the new keyword), they get allocated on the heap. It is the responsibility of the programmer to delete the allocated instance. Now, you as a C++ programmer might be well aware of the consequences if you fail to delete. So scary ... memory leaks!!!

© Vivek Ragunathan 2016
V. Ragunathan, *C++/CLI Primer*, DOI 10.1007/978-1-4842-2367-3_6

Value Types and Reference Types are a part of the managed world. They behave as the CLI dictates, the prime doctrine being to have a common base type: System::Object. The following are the methods exposed by System::Object:

Method Name	Return Type	Accessibility
Equals	bool	public
GetType	Type	public
ToString	System::String^	public
GetHashCode	int	public
Finalize	—	protected
MemberwiseClone	System::Object^	protected
ReferenceEquals	bool	public static

From a quick look, it should be obvious that these listed in the table are methods/operations that the runtime would require on any object; hence, System::Object. And so is every type derived from System::Object.

Value Types are derived from System::ValueType, which is further derived from System::Object. The value types are always allocated on the stack. However, there are times when they are transported to the heap. Although we associate Value Types to being allocated on the stack, what is more important about Value Types is the value/copy semantics.

When a variable a of some value type is assigned to a variable b of the same type, it is copied memberwise to the other object, which is in contrast to a reference type. In the case of reference types, an object would have been created on the heap prior to assignment b = a, which both a and b would be referring to.

In C++/CLI, all primitive types are value types. User-defined values can also be defined, which is discussed in detail in a later section.

Primitive Types Mapping

Data Type Name	Type	Keyword
Integer	System.Int32	int
Double	System.Double	double
Character (2 bytes)	System.Char	char
Character (1 Byte)	System.Byte	byte
Boolean	System.Boolean	bool

The preceding table list is not extensive.

© Vivek Ragunathan 2016

V. Ragunathan, *C++/CLI Primer*, DOI 10.1007/978-1-4842-2367-3_7

The following is the way primitive value types are declared and used:

```
void InSomeMethod()
{
        // You may also used int keyword instead.
        System::Int32 oddNumber = 1;
        CallAnotherMethod(oddNumber);

        // You may also used char keyword instead.
        System::Char character = 'A';
        CallMethod3(character);
}
```

enums

The following is a typical declaration of a managed enumeration:

```
enum class Color
{
        Black,
        Red,
        Blue,
        Green
}
```

The first thing about managed enumerations that differentiates them from the unmanaged enumerations is that managed enumerations must have names—for instance, Color. Managed enumerations are scoped, which means that values must be accessed using their enclosing enumeration name: two enumerations can have the same value name. The default underlying type of an enumeration is integer; but of course, that can be chosen among signed and unsigned integers (int, short, long), char, or bool.

The following is an example of a managed enumeration whose underlying type is `bool`:

```
enum class Response : bool
{
        Positive = true,
        Negative = false,
        OK = true,
        Cancel = false,
        Yes,
        No
}
```

Anonymous managed enumerations are not supported.

User-Defined Value Types

User-defined value types can be defined by decorating a class or struct with the value qualifier.

```
public value struct Person
{
private:
        String^ name;
        int age;
...
};
```

Bear in mind that unlike C#, it is not the struct keyword that makes it a value type. Just like C++, struct and class in C++/CLI differ only by default visibility assumed by its members. It is the value qualifier that makes it a value type. Likewise, it is the ref qualifier that makes it a reference type.

© Vivek Ragunathan 2016
V. Ragunathan, *C++/CLI Primer*, DOI 10.1007/978-1-4842-2367-3_8

The following is the way user-defined value types are declared and used:

```
value struct DateTimeInfo
{
        private: System::Int32 Year;
        private: System::char Month;
        private: System::char Date;

        // NOTE: Cannot declare default ctor in structs.

        public: DateTimeInfo(int year, char mon, char date)
        {
        }

        public: int GetYear()
        {
                return this->Year;
        }

        public: int GetMonth()
        {
                return static_cast<int>(this->Month);
        }

        public: int GetDate()
        {
                return static_cast<int>(this->Date);
        }

};
```

Reference Types

Reference types are classes and structs decorated with the ref qualifier. Instances of Reference Types are always allocated on the heap. Here comes the interesting part. This heap is not the same heap where your native types are allocated—the unmanaged heap. This is a different area called the **managed heap**. The native type or code has no idea or direct reach to the managed heap. So then, how do we allocate on the managed heap? Is it by using the new keyword? If so, how does the new keyword know where to allocate then? To get around, there is a newer keyword called gcnew.

Keyword new allocates on the native heap, and gcnew allocates on the managed heap.

© Vivek Ragunathan 2016
V. Ragunathan, *C++/CLI Primer*, DOI 10.1007/978-1-4842-2367-3_9

Examples and code snippets are not appropriate yet, but just consider the following for now:

```
reference_data_type objRef = gcnew appropriate ctor of
                                  reference_data_type
```

This is the conventional way of creating a managed object in C++\CLI. As mentioned earlier, the instance is created on the managed heap. The accessor for that instance is called the object reference (objRef in the preceding code) or handle, and it is allocated on the stack.

Per C++\CLI convention, a reference to an object is called a handle. However, let's stick to (object) reference, which is the widely used term in the managed world. The term **object reference** must not in any way be related to the C++ reference. Therefore, the word **reference** in the rest of the book refers to the managed object reference only, unless and until explicitly distinguished.

The instance cannot be accessed without the object reference. In essence, object references are address holders. However, they are not like native pointers. Object references are type aware, polymorphic, and exhibit the type's behavior. References do not follow pointer semantics. In other words, references cannot be cast to any type desired or moved by incrementing or decrementing the address. So, they are much more intelligent address holders.

An assignment of an object reference to another is a shallow copy, in this case, the address. Hence, there can be more than one reference to the instance on the managed heap. With multiple references to an object, memory management is a C++ programmer's nightmare. Unless C++/CLI doesn't offer a better way to deal with the memory management, it would be no better or no more powerful than C++.

Enter . . . GC, aka Garbage Collection.

Garbage Collection Intro

The managed programming model does not expect the programmer to perform manual memory management. It is not required that the programmer write code such as delete objRef to deallocate and return back the memory that was allocated. Spare our poor programmers. The CLR is very smart and reclaims memory through a process called Garbage Collection, and the component of the CLR that performs automatic memory management is the Garbage Collector. The abbreviation GC is used interchangeably for the process and the component (depending on the context).

© Vivek Ragunathan 2016

V. Ragunathan, *C++/CLI Primer*, DOI 10.1007/978-1-4842-2367-3_10

The Garbage Collector reclaims only those instances that are not reachable, namely, for which you lose the object references (such as objRef mentioned previously). If the object reference goes out of scope, or if it was assigned null, the instance it was referring to cannot be reached through this reference anymore. In other words, for an instance memory to be reclaimed by the GC, there must be no outstanding references. This is the most compelling feature of the .NET. Programmers are now free of the burden to write code to delete the memory they allocate, which has been the tough schooling they have gone through in the several years of programming. Beware! Too much freedom results in chaos. Even with GC, memory has to be allocated wisely because indisciplined allocations will degrade application performance. This is one of the fundamental differences between native and managed worlds.

Although GC is responsible only for deallocating the memory, it is not so for the associated resource. For instance, if you have opened a connection with a database, the GC is not responsible for closing the connection; instead, it is responsible only for reclaiming the memory allocated for the connection object.

Declaring and Consuming a Managed Class

With the basics you learned in the previous chapters, it is time to see stuff that works. The following is a snippet of a C++\CLI class (see Listing 11-1).

© Vivek Ragunathan 2016
V. Ragunathan, *C++/CLI Primer*, DOI 10.1007/978-1-4842-2367-3_11

Listing 11-1.

```
ref class Directory
{
        public: Directory();
        // Creates an instance with the current directory
           path
        public: Directory(System::String^ filePath);
        // Creates an instance with the specified
           directory path
        public: File^ GetFile(System::String^ fileName);
        // Assume File is another managed class

        public: cli::array<System::String^, 1>^ GetFiles();
        public: cli::array<System::String^, 1>^ GetFiles
               (System::String^ filter);
        public: System::Void DeleteFile(System::String^
               fileName);

        // imagine a few other methods....
};
```

Listing 11-1 is the typical way of declaring a managed class in C++\CLI. The ref keyword preceding the class keyword distinguishes it as a managed class and as a candidate for getting allocated on the managed heap. Let's see how to create an instance of the preceding class:

```
Directory^ sysDir = gcnew Directory();
```

The caret (^) symbol specifies that the variable sysDir is a reference to a managed object. You can call public methods, and you can copy the reference to another reference variable:

```
Directory^ sysDir2 = sysDir;
```

Now, sysDir and sysDir2 both refer to the same instance. It is not required to explicitly delete the object as you would have to do with C++. The memory reclamation part is now a responsibility of the .NET runtime (GC). This is really a big relief for the programmer.

The effect of calling delete on the instance (delete sysDir) is discussed in Chapter 12.

The following is the way you invoke methods on the Directory instance:

```
File^ someFile = sysDir->GetFile("SomeFile.TXT");
```

Consider the following method:

```
System::Void UseSysDir(Directory^ dirObjRef)
{
        cli::array<system::String^,>^ files = dirObjRef->
                                              GetFiles();
        // do something with files.
}
```

The object reference now can be passed to methods as parameters and can be accessed the same way inside the methods too. All of the references are to the same instance on the managed heap. There is no copy construction involved anywhere because a copy of the object is not created. It is similar to passing pointers in C++. In case you need to create a copy, you should derive your class from the System::IClonable and implement the Clone() method. The actual depth of the copy depends on your implementation. Each inner object may or may not require a Clone method in turn. It might be very hard at first for a C++ programmer to digest the practice of passing around references for the same object, instead of implementing and using a copy constructor. I guarantee that in due course you will definitely learn to appreciate that programming with objects on the heap and the memory reclamation by garbage collector is a different model altogether.

Consider the following code:

```
Directory^ CreateDirectory(System::String^ dirPath)
{
        // some code to checks...if you want (just to
           make the method look big) !!!
        Directory^ dirObj = gcnew Directory(dirPath);
        // some other code ...
        return dirObj;
}
```

An instance of the Directory class is created, and a reference to the allocated instance is returned. After returning, the dirObj will no longer refer to the object on the heap. It is the responsibility of the calling method to grab the returned reference and preserve it so that GC does not mark the object as orphaned or garbage. When there is at least one direct or indirect object reference for a particular object, the GC will not attempt to reclaim the memory being consumed by that object.

Boxing/ Unboxing

As we saw earlier, Value Types are allocated on the stack. There are times when they are present on the managed heap. For instance, when a method takes a System::Object (the mother of all managed types) as the parameter for, say, printing the contents, an object is allocated on the heap with the value of the Value Type copied to it. This process is called **boxing**.

The following is sample code that shows boxing:

```
int i =100;
System::Object^ boxObj = safe_cast<System::Object^>(i);
// Boxing
```

© Vivek Ragunathan 2016
V. Ragunathan, *C++/CLI Primer*, DOI 10.1007/978-1-4842-2367-3_12

Or see the following:

```
void PrintContents(Object^ objRef)
{
        // blah, blah blah....
        Console::WriteLine("Contents: {0}",
        objRef->ToString());
}

InSomeMethod()
{
        int i = 100;
        PrintContents(i); // i is boxed
}
```

The opposite of boxing is called **unboxing**: it is retrieving the value of the instance from the heap and loading it on the variable on the stack.

```
void Unbox()
{
        System::Object^ integerObj = safe_cast<System::
                                        Object^>(100); // box

        int i = safe_cast<int>(integerObj); // unbox
}
```

Apart from boxing, a Value Type resides on the heap when it is part of a reference type object.

Boxing/unboxing should be obvious for primitive types. How is it dealt with in the case of user-defined Value Types? Consider the following Value Type:

```
value struct Person
{
        private: String^ name;
        private: int age;
        private: double weight;
        // ... rest of the code
}
```

Let's first consider unboxing. When `Person` object is unboxed, the object is reconstructed on the stack. That means, apart from object metadata, the `Person` fields get allocated on the stack just like the primitive types. The reverse happens in the case of boxing.

Boxing and unboxing are applicable only for value types.

Object Destruction

This is a very fuzzy but interesting area.

In C++, a destructor is a language construct to perform cleanup on the object after its scope of use and before its memory is reclaimed. Destruction in C++ is deterministic, meaning you know exactly when an object has begun its course of destruction. The destructor for an object allocated on the stack is called when it goes out of scope. For an object allocated on the heap, it is called when delete is called. If you fail to call delete (after the formal consumption of the object), the destructor is never called, and the memory held by the object is not released—memory leaks. Now we know that story.

© Vivek Ragunathan 2016
V. Ragunathan, *C++/CLI Primer*, DOI 10.1007/978-1-4842-2367-3_13

On the contrary, managed object destruction is non-deterministic, meaning the GC will reclaim object memory at an arbitrary time (not definitely right after the scope of use) and on an arbitrary thread. Ideally, there are no destructors for managed objects (implemented in most other .NET languages) because the destruction of such objects is not deterministic. C++/CLI is a class apart.

When you are done using an object, there are two ways available to cleanup—dispose and finalize.

Cleanup Dispose

There are times when you know the scope of the object use (lifetime). In such cases, you can invoke an explicit call on the object to perform cleanup. Per the .NET recommendation, you can perform an explicit cleanup by invoking the Dispose method on the object (if the object implements System::IDisposable). The dispose method is intended solely for object/resource cleanup, while the object memory is reclaimed during GC at a later and arbitrary point in time.

Cleanup Finalize

There is another, but last chance, in the lifetime of an object to perform cleanup, even after you have given up all the references to the object. That is when the object gets finalized. When the garbage collector finds an orphaned or garbage object, it adds that object to a special queue (called the **Finalization Queue**) *if the object implements the* Finalize *method*. A dedicated thread, called the **Finalizer Thread**, calls the Finalize() method—also called the **finalizer** method—on each of the queued objects. This process is called **Finalization**. The Finalize() is the last method call on an object in its lifetime; after that, the object vanishes. Bear in mind that resource cleanup can only be **attempted** in the finalize method. So you must be prepared for the worst.

The Finalize method is called at an arbitrary point in time long after the object is reachable from your code. There is no order in which the finalizers are called. If object A contains object B, it is not necessary that the finalizer for object B be called first. The order is not guaranteed. Then what good is a finalizer for? Theoretically, it is for releasing unmanaged resources that the object might contain. *Unmanaged objects are not collected by the GC.* They exist until they are explicitly released.

Finalization is a very involved process in the lifetime of an object, the details of which are intricate and outside the scope of this book. For the most part, you can consider it as an undocumented feature. That is to say, you should never put your code in a situation to rely on the finalization for resource cleanup.

Implementing a finalizer method is targeted only for particular classes of objects, specifically, those that rely on native resources such as OS handles and so forth. During the course of evolution of the CLR, even such classes of objects are recommended to implement SafeHandle. In other words, implementing a finalizer is highly discouraged.

Implementing a finalizer has indirect consequence of affecting the application performance because the GC cannot reclaim the memory right away in its course of collection but defers until after running through the finalizer.

So, what would happen if you chose to Dispose and the Finalize method is also called on the object (assuming the object implements the Finalize method)? Or what happens when Dispose is called multiple times? It could be disastrous to clean up an object more than once. So how do we then avoid redundant cleanups? .NET recommends the Dispose Pattern. The idea is to prevent detect and avoid Dispose-ing an object more than once and also prevent the Finalize from being invoked if you have already called Dispose.

The garbage collector is exposed via the System.GC class.

The following is the Dispose pattern implementation snippet:

```
ref class MyDisposableClass : IDisposable
{
        private: bool disposed;

        // Ctors, and other methods

        public: void Dispose()
        {
                // Do clean up on the managed/unmanaged
                   parts
                // of the object

                if (!disposed)
                {
                        Dispose(true);

                        // If the Dispose is called, then
                           suppress
                        // from being finalized

                        System::GC::SupressFinalize(this);
                }
        }

        public: void Finalize()
        {
                // If the object is getting finalized, then
                // pass false so that any managed object
                   access
                // is not made; since objects are finalized
                // as per their hierarchies and
                   dependencies.
                // Hence, only unmanaged cleanup, if any.

                Dispose(false);
        }
```

```
protected: void Dispose(bool safe2FreeManaged)
{
        // This method will be called with
           safe2FreeManaged = true when
        // Object.Dispose is explicitly called, in
           which case it is
        // safe to access and cleanup managed
           resources.
        // This method will be called with
           safe2FreeManaged = false from
        // the finalizer and may not be not safe
           to even access managed
        // resources.

        if (safe2FreeManaged)
        {
                InternalDispose();
        }
        // code to release unmanaged resources-
           COM objects etc

}

private: void InternalDispose()
{
        // Actual clean up happens here !!!

}
};
```

The GC.SupressFinalize method, when called for the desired object, suppresses the finalizer from calling the Finalize method from being called on the object.

To appeal to the C++ programmers, C++/CLI wisely reuses the existing syntax to preserve the concepts and the practices. In C++\CLI, it is not required to explicitly derive from System::IDisposable and implement the Dispose method. Instead, the C++ destructor syntax is analogous to the InternalDispose method (see MyDisposableClass class). When you implement a destructor using the conventional C++ destructor syntax (~ClassName), the compiler automatically derives the class from System::IDisposable and implements the Dispose pattern for you. The skeleton of the Dispose pattern is just a boilerplate, which the compiler injects on your behalf if you provide the cleanup logic via the destructor.

If there is no destructor for a class, then it is not derived from System.IDisposable, and C++/CLI assumes that you made a conscious decision not to implement the Dispose pattern. Because the destructor syntax has been chosen for the Dispose method, the semantics is also preserved. That means Dispose is automatically called when the object falls out of scope. Whereas other .NET languages lack in this aspect—destructor—C++/CLI excels in exercising a hold on the object lifetime, particularly the cleanup. This is one of the distinguishing features in C++/CLI.

Like the destructor or the Dispose method, the Finalize method can also be defined syntactically with a !{ClassName}; instead of a ~.

Here is the refined MyDisposableClass class:

```
ref class MyDisposableClass
{

        // Destructor (Dispose Method)
        ~MyDisposableClass()
        {
                // perform resource cleanup
        }

        // Finalizer
        !MyDisposableClass()
        {
                // Perform cleanup, only for unmanaged
                    resources.
        }
};
```

Note that C++/CLI implements the Dispose pattern for you, letting you focus on the cleanup logic.

The following is likely a way that C++\CLI implements the
Dispose pattern for you:

```
// This method is called by the compiler implemented
// IDisposable::Dipose and Object::Finalize methods.

Dispose(bool safe2FreeMgd)
{
        if(safe2FreeMgd)
        {
                try
                {
                        //call the dtor code (~ClassName)
                }
                finally
                {
                        // This call to the GC will suppress
                        // the class from getting finalized
                        GC::SuppressFinalize(this);
                }
        }
        else
        {
                //call the finalizer code (!ClassName)
        }

        // Call BaseClass::Dispose(safe2FreeMgd);
}
```

Scope of a Managed Object

Consider the MyDisposableClass class that we saw earlier. It is a reference type. So what does falling *out of scope* mean for a reference type? To the .NET in general, it does not make sense. However, in C++/CLI, because it is related to a destructor, it does make sense.

© Vivek Ragunathan 2016

V. Ragunathan, *C++/CLI Primer*, DOI 10.1007/978-1-4842-2367-3_14

Now, take a look at this:

```
System::Void SomeMethod(if you need parameters)
{
        Directory dirObj;
        dirObj.DeleteFile("System.TXT");
        // Call other methods you need.........
        // dirObj's dtor (or rather Dispose) is
        // dirObj falls out of scope.
}
```

Unlike earlier where we gcnew a managed object and declare the variable with a ^, the dirObj in the preceding code does neither. It resembles how in C++ you would declare an object to be allocated on the stack.

The Directory instance referred by the dirObj variable is actually allocated on the managed heap, but it is declared in a way (similar to C++) to be Disposed when dirObj goes out of scope. The compiler automatically inserts the call to the Dispose method or the destructor call. Also, notice that the members are accessed by a.(dot) operator instead of a -> operator. This resembles as if the object is allocated on the stack and mirrors the C++ stack-based object semantics. Isn't that cool? This is also one of the cool features that provide backward compatibility for the syntax. It shows that the language designers have respect for the habits of C++ programmers.

Although the dirObj resembles a stack-object, the associated reference type object is never allocated on the stack. It is allocated on the managed heap.

C++/CLI does not support declaring destructors or the Dispose method and the Finalize method for Value Types. It is not a limitation but a (language) design choice.

Mixed Mode

Mixed-mode programming is the absolute power of C++\CLI. That is why C++\CLI is the superior and mightiest of all programming languages on the .NET.

The relation between C++ and C++/CLI is similar to the one between C++ and C. You can do C programming in C++. In the same sense, you can do unmanaged C++ programming in C++\CLI without using any of the managed features, not even a managed class. Of course, there is no good reason to do so. Also, you can do pure managed programming without using any of the unmanaged practices. You can also do mixed-mode programming, which means you can write an application that has both managed and unmanaged classes interacting with each other. That means there can be an object on the managed heap and another on the unmanaged heap, and they can invoke calls on one another. This is the hallmark of programming with C++/CLI and has real world use cases. C++/CLI wasn't made for fun, nor is it a pet language.

For instance, imagine your team had developed a hi-fi image processing or math library in C++. You are moving your applications to the .NET platform. Let's say you do not have enough budget/time to rewrite your library in C#

© Vivek Ragunathan 2016
V. Ragunathan, *C++/CLI Primer*, DOI 10.1007/978-1-4842-2367-3_15

(or VB.NET). The simplest approach is to recompile your existing code with C++\CLI and write a (managed) wrapper so that they can be used by any .NET programming language. The time and effort to write a managed wrapper compared to the effort of rewriting and testing it is orders of magnitude less.

The following is a managed class that interacts with an unmanaged object:

```
ref class ManagedClass
{
        private: UnmanagedClass* unmgdPtr;

        public: ManagedClass(UnmanagedClass* unmgdClassPtr)
        {
                // similar to _ASSERTE(..); see nullptr
                    usage.

                System::Diagnostics::Debug::Assert
                (unmgdClassPtr != nullptr);
                this->unmgdPtr = unmgdClassPtr;
        }

        public: // Some methods that use the unmgdPtr

};

class UnmanagedClass
{
        public: UnmanagedClass()
        {
        }

        public: void SomeUnmgdMethod()
        {
        }

        // imagine a ton of other public methods


};
```

Likewise, an unmanaged class can bear a managed reference and can invoke methods on it. Unlike a managed class holding the pointer to unmanaged, it cannot directly have the reference; instead, it is done the following way:

```
// ref class Managed Class - Some managed class

class UnmanagedClass
{
        private: gcroot<ManagedClass^> mgdRef;
        public: UnmanagedClass(ManagedClass^ mgdClassRef)
        {
                Debug::Assert(mgdClassRef != nullptr);
                this->mgdRef = mgdClassRef;
        }

        // Methods that use mgdRef and invoke methods:
           mgd->SomeMethod();


};
```

The keyword **gcroot** is a means for the managed code to hold a reference to a managed instance. The gcroot is itself an unmanaged entity. An instance of gcroot<managed> can be a statically or dynamically allocated member inside the unmanaged class; gcroot is what we call the gray area of the .NET—neither managed nor unmanaged.

Equality and Identity

Two managed objects are said to be equal if their values are same. The System::Object's Equals method can be used to test equivalence. The Equals is an instance virtual method and can be overridden in a derived class/struct because equality of compound objects depends on the type. Two managed objects are said to be identical if their references point to the same object on the heap. The System::Object's ReferenceEquals static method can be used to test identity.

The crux of CLI is the importance of a type of an object. Unlike unmanaged objects, managed objects know who they are, right from the moment they spring to life, either on the stack or on the heap. The type information of an object can be obtained by using the typeid operator and using System::Object's GetType method for the instances. The importance of the type can be realized if you try the GetType in the constructor. You will be surprised that it returns the type of the instance being constructed. For instance, see the following case:

© Vivek Ragunathan 2016

V. Ragunathan, *C++/CLI Primer*, DOI 10.1007/978-1-4842-2367-3_16

```
ref class SomeClass
{
        public: int X;
        public: int Y;
        public: SomeClass(int x, int y)
        {
                **Console::WriteLine("Type - {0}", this
                ->GetType()->ToString());**

                Method();
        }
        public: virtual void Method()
        {
                Console::WriteLine("SomeClass::Method");
        }
};

ref class SomeOtherClass : public SomeClass
{
        public: SomeOtherClass(int x, int y)
                : SomeClass(x, y)
        {
        }
        public: virtual void Method() override
        {
                Console::WriteLine("SomeOtherClass::
                Method");
        }
};
```

The highlighted Console::WriteLine will output the type
of the instance being created and not always SomeClass. That
is, if an instance of SomeOtherClass is created, you will see
SomeOtherClass in the output. Also, you will be thrilled to
know that the virtual calls in the constructor are directed
to the appropriate overrides. This, of course, is not recommended usage and is not a good discipline. It is just being
pointed out to understand the importance of a Type.

Abstract Classes

As you might already know, an abstract class is one whose sole purpose is to act as a base class only, which means such a class cannot be instantiated.

In C++, the abstract class is declared only by declaring one or more pure virtual functions. C++ does not provide a direct language construct such as a keyword.

C++/CLI provides the abstract keyword for declaring abstract classes. Also, methods can be decorated with the abstract keyword, in which case the containing class must also be decorated the same way. The following are explanatory code snippets:

```
ref class AnAbstractClass abstract
{
      // ctor and other methods that have method bodies

};
```

© Vivek Ragunathan 2016

V. Ragunathan, *C++/CLI Primer*, DOI 10.1007/978-1-4842-2367-3_17

or

```
// Cannot create instances of AnotherAbstractClass

ref class AnotherAbstractClass abstract
{

// member declaration
// ctor
// methods with bodies


public: virtual void SomeMethod(int x) abstract;

// Making a method abstract requires the class to
   decorated with
// the abstract keyword.

};

ref class DerivedFromAnotherAbstractClass : public
AnotherAbstractClass
{
        // This is the overriding implementation of
           SomeMethod. Preceding
        // virtual keyword and the override suffix keyword
           mandatory to
        // denote that we intend to override SomeMethod

        public: virtual void SomeMethod(int x) override
        {
                // impl
        }
};
```

Nullptr

When a C++ pointer is NULL, it does not point to any location in the memory. Similarly, when an object reference does not point to any object, its value is nullptr. The nullptr is a keyword in C++\CLI. However, unlike NULL, nullptr is safer and is not a type. A NULL at the end of the day is an integer constant. Because nullptr is not a type, no type operations can be done on nullptr—sizeof(nullptr), throw nullptr, and so forth will all result in compiler errors.

- A nullptr can be assigned to an object reference as part of the declaration or later.

```
Directory^ dirObjRef = nullptr;
```

- A nullptr can be explicitly assigned even when the reference is referring to some other object.

© Vivek Ragunathan 2016
V. Ragunathan, *C++/CLI Primer*, DOI 10.1007/978-1-4842-2367-3_18

```
Directory^ dirObjRef = gcnew Directory(some directory
                       path string);

dirObjRef->DeleteFile("SomeFile.TXT");
```

```
// possible candidate for GC, if there are no other
   references for the object
```

```
dirObjRef = nullptr;
```

- A nullptr can be used for comparing with an object reference, but other arithmetic operators (+, –, >, <, etc.) are not allowed.

  - if (dirObjRef == nullptr) { *throw some exception or as you wish....* }

  - if (dirObjRef != nullptr) { .... }

- A nullptr can be passed to methods as parameters and can return values too.

```
dirObjRef->GetFile(nullptr);
```

and

```
File^ GetFile("SomeFile.TXT")
{
      // ......
      // if file not found
      return nullptr;
}
```

- A nullptr can be assigned to a managed reference, interior pointer (discussed later), or a native pointer.

Declaring Properties

There is an easier and very elegant way in C++\CLI for writing get/set methods. A Property is a getter and/or setter construct exposed on a class. The accessibility of the getter and setter of the property can be chosen as per one's needs. For instance, it is possible to write a property that has a public getter but private or protected setter.

Let's say we have a Status class, and it has a few parameters: some of which are writable, some only readable, and some both readable and writable. Here is how to implement Status class with the above mentioned properties:

© Vivek Ragunathan 2016
V. Ragunathan, *C++/CLI Primer*, DOI 10.1007/978-1-4842-2367-3_19

```cpp
public ref class Status
{
    private: float pressureValue;
    private: int temperatureValue;
    private: DateTime recordDateTime;

    public: Status()
    {
        this->RecordTime = DateTime::Now;
    }

    // This property value is readable and writable

    public: property float Pressure
    {
        float get()
        {
            return  this->pressureValue;
        }

        void set(float pval)
        {
            // Do checks on pval, if required

            this->pressureValue = pval;
        }
    }

    // This property value is readable, but writable only
    //    derived classes

    public: property float Temperature
    {
        float get()
        {
            return this->temperatureValue;
        }

        protected: void set(float tval)
        {
            this->temperatureValue = tval;
        }
    }
```

```cpp
// This property is read only [writable within the class]

public: property DateTime RecordTime
{
      DateTime get()
      {
            return this->recordDateTime;
      }

      private: void set(DateTime dtval)
      {
            this->recordDateTime = dtval;
      }
}
};
```

Users of the Status class write code as shown in the following:

```cpp
ref class UserClass
{
      // Create the Status class object (statusObject)
         in one of the methods.


      public: void LogPressure()
      {
            Console::WriteLine("Pressure: {0}",
            statusObject->Pressure);
      }
      public: void SetPressure(float pval)
      {
            statusObject->Pressure = pval;
      }
};
```

Properties are an elegant way of reading and writing data members of a class. Accessing the data members of a class via properties instead of conventional get/set methods enhances the aesthetics of the client code.

Properties can be declared on a class, struct, or interface. Therefore, they can be virtual: either get or set or both. Properties can be static too, and the static applies to the property as a whole.

Besides data member properties, there is something called an **Indexed property**. It is essentially a property that provides an indexing operator for the class. The indexing can be multidimensional. For instance, consider a class named Manager that has an array of Reportees as a member:

```
using namespace System;

public ref class Reportee
{
private: String^ reporteeName;

public: Reportee(String^ name)
{
        this->Name = name;
}

public: property String^ Name
{
        String^ get()
        {
                return this->reporteeName;
        }

        private: void set(String^ name)
        {
                this->reporteeName = name;
        }
}
};
```

```cpp
public ref class Manager
{

        // Assume reporteeList to be populated in the ctor
private: cli::array<Reportee^>^ reporteeList;

                // Readable Indexed property [writable
                   only by derived classes].
                // Indexed property must have the name as
                   default. It can take any type as
                // parameter that will be used as a index
                   to fetch the corresponding value
                // from one of the data structures that
                   is a member of the class like
                // reporteeList here in this class.

public: property Reportee^ default[int]
{
        Reportee^ get(int index)
        {
                if (index >= 0 && index < reporteeList->
                            Length)
                {
                        return this->reporteeList[index];
                }

                return nullptr;
        }

        protected: void set(int index, Reportee^ robj)
        {
                if (index >= 0 && index < reporteeList-
                            >Length && robj != nullptr)
                {
                        this->reporteeList[index] = robj;
                }
        }
}
}
```

```
// A readonly non-indexed property

public: property int ReporteesCount
{
        int get()
        {
                return this->reporteeList->Length;
        }
}

// Other methods
};
```

Here is how you can use the property on the Manager class:

```
ref class SomeUserClass
{
        public: void LogReporteeInfo(Manager^ mgr)
        {
                for (int i = 0; i < mgr->ReporteesCount; ++i)
                {
                        // Using the indexed property on
                           Manager

                        Console::WriteLine("Reportee {0}:
                        {1}", i + 1, mgr[i]->Name);
                }
        }
};
```

With the use of properties, methods such as GetSomeValue and SetSomeValue(Value) are replaced by the short, sweet, and elegant obj->*PropertyName* and obj->*PropertyName* = *SomeValue* syntax. It is recommended very much that properties be used for only getting and setting the corresponding entity of the class and to avoid other unrelated operations.

Strings

There has never been a type for string literals in C++. For instance, the type of 2 is `int`, and the type of s is `char`. Likewise, there is no inherent type for "Hello World" in the language. It can be accessed as `char *` or `const char *`. But it is not the native type of the string literal. In other words, the language does not have a singular way of associating a type to the literal. There is no keyword in the language for a string like there is for `int` or `char` or `bool`. In many ways, string is not a first-class citizen in the language.

The .NET (CLR) associates `System.String` as the type for strings. C# offers a `string` keyword too. Methods can be directly invoked on string literals—"Hello World".Length gives 12. This is not so in C++.

In the later years of evolution, the language provided the efficient and easy-to-use STL (Standard Template Library), which has a `std::string` class for creating and managing strings. Even `std::string` is not the native type of a string. Therefore, when "Hello World" is passed as an argument for a method

```
int StringTest(std::string);
```

© Vivek Ragunathan 2016

V. Ragunathan, *C++/CLI Primer*, DOI 10.1007/978-1-4842-2367-3_20

it requires a conversion (using the ctor).

If you had high hopes on C++\CLI to recognize a string as a first-class citizen, you would be disappointed to know that there is still no type for string literals. However, because C++\ CLI is a secular (managed/unmanaged) programming language, there are some interesting things to be noted.

String literals in C++\CLI have the flexibility of associating themselves with (the closest) managed or unmanaged types, based on the context; and of course, managed types take higher precedence. So, "Hello World" can be treated as System::String or const char * or char *. Let's learn that with an example:

```
int StringTest(const char *);
int StringTest(System::Object^ strObject);
int StringTest(System::String^ clrString);
int StringTest(std::string stdString);
```

Which of the preceding methods do you think the following call will bind to?

```
StringTest("Hello World");
```

The previous call will bind to the System::String^ overload. As I said earlier, managed types are given higher precedence. In the absence of the System::String^ overload, the call will be bound to the overload with System::Object^ as the argument. The unmanaged const char * will be considered in the absence of both of the managed types.

Even among managed types, only those that are found closest to the adopted string literals are considered; when none are found compatible, the const char * overload takes precedence. Types that require conversion (using conversion operators or constructors) assume lower precedence, which is the case with the std::string overload.

So what do you think will happen with the following line of code—compilation error, runtime error, or runs fine?

```
int hc = "Hello World"->GetHashCode();
```

Guesses apart, the preceding line of code will result in a compilation error. Now don't try to replace the -> with . (dot):. The compiler finds no context like a method call to match the type of the string literal to an existing type, which should convince you that there is no inherent compiler type for string literals—period. All the different flavors of type matching for string literals may help us build a C++ world where "Hello World"s are one day System::String. Therefore, try to write code (as much as possible) that binds to System::String.

Arrays—Not [] But cli:: array<T^>

A great relief that C++/CLI brings for C++ programmers is maintaining arrays. The programmer had to be aware of the array boundaries, range check during access, and other such things. There is an array type that comes with C++\CLI. It is a language-defined type. It is not a keyword, although it is a reserved word. Any managed array is an instance of the cli::array class, which by itself is a reference type and extends the System::Array type. It can hold a fixed number of value or reference types; fixed refers the fact that the size of the array is determined at creation time and cannot be changed after creating, although the array itself can be created dynamically at runtime.

© Vivek Ragunathan 2016
V. Ragunathan, *C++/CLI Primer*, DOI 10.1007/978-1-4842-2367-3_21

The following are the typical ways of allocating an array of integers:

```
// Allocates the array of size 10 initialized with zeroes

cli::array<int>^ intArray = gcnew cli::array<int>(10);

// Allocates an array of size 10 and initializes
// the first 5 elements but can initialize all too

cli::array<int>^ intArray = gcnew cli::array<int>(10)
                            { 0, 1, 2 , 3, 4 };

// Allocates an array of size 10 initialized with zeroes,
// later fills them with some values

cli::array<int><int>^ intArray = gcnew cli::array<int>^(10);
for (int i = 0; i < 10; ++i)
{
   intArray[i] = i + 1;
}

// An array of reference types

// Note the ^ for the type held by the array.

cli::array<SomeRefType^>^ arrayOfRefs = gcnew cli::array
                                <SomeRefType^>(10);
for (int  i = 0; i &lt; 10; ++i)
{
      arrayOfRefs[i] = gcnew SomeRefType();
}
```

- The individual values of an array are boxed if they are value types.

- Array index is zero based.

- The array type has methods for accessing and manipulating the contents of the array.

- All operations on the array are bound checked. Any access beyond the maximum size of the array results in an exception—*Index out of range*.

- Arrays get allocated only on the heap; hence, an array of value types gets all its values boxed to the heap.

A cli::array in C++\CLI is the emissary of the Array type in the BCL (Base Class Library). For dynamically growing arrays, use System.Collections.ArrayList or any of the generic collections in the BCL.

A Second Look at GC

The following is a brief and conventional description of how a garbage collector works:

> *Garbage collector is the part of a runtime that takes care of automatic memory management. That means it is not only responsible for reclaiming memory but allocating it too. You could say allocating is the other side of the coin. If you visualize the managed heap as an ice tray with a huge number of sequential ice molds (holes) where an empty mold denotes a garbage or unreferred object, then the garbage collector as part of memory reclamation moves all empty molds between the occupied ones such that the occupied molds are kept contiguous. This is called compaction. Actually, the moving of molds happens the other way—live objects are moved to the first available empty spots.*

© Vivek Ragunathan 2016
V. Ragunathan, *C++/CLI Primer*, DOI 10.1007/978-1-4842-2367-3_22

Compaction prevents the managed heap from getting fragmented over time, which is one of the theoritical breakpoints for an unmanaged application. The effect of compaction on allocation is very fast, unlike C++ runtime in which a block memory of appropriate size has to be looked up. The allocation pointer on the managed heap is always at the start of the free memory. But because compaction relocates a live object, the garbage collector will have to update all of its references in the application. For instance, if an instance (live object) "X" is moved from address "A" to address "B," then variables that are currently referring to "X" at "A" will have to be updated to point to "B."

Let's stop there for a second and talk about the .NET GC. The .NET GC has special requirements beyond the preceding conventional description.

C++/CLI is one of the languages that run on the .NET CLR. That means all the power of the language comes from the runtime—particularly the mixed mode. Now imagine that in a particular mixed-mode scenario, a piece of managed code makes a call to an unmanaged function passing the address of a managed object—array/buffer—which the unmanaged function fills with some data (e.g., image pixels or data from a stream, etc.). If a GC is triggered during the time when the call to the unmanaged function is in progress but not returned yet, then the compaction is likely to move the managed reference to the buffer elsewhere, away from the location that the unmanaged function would be writing to. If that is allowed to happen, the application will end up in a corrupted state.

The GC cannot perform any updates in the unmanaged code. Remember, the GC operates only on the managed heap. Of course, the integrity of the managed–unmanaged call should be preserved at any cost pre- and post-GC. One wild way to resolve this conundrum is to not move the managed object (array/buffer) during GC so that the unmanaged function is transparent to GC. Well, that's what it is: enter `pin_ptr`.

pin_ptr<T>

A `pin_ptr<T>`, which when instantiated for a managed type/instance, **pins** the instance from being moved during garbage collection (particularly compaction).

Just as an `interior_ptr` is a superset of a native pointer, a `pin_ptr` is a superset of an `interior_ptr`.

If `pin_ptr` were let loose, then one could pin every other managed object and render the GC literally useless. Hence, a set of rules is imposed on a `pin_ptr`:

1. If a member of an object is pinned, the entire object is pinned. An object cannot have a scattered layout. Its members have to be packed logically contiguous, although not necessarily physically. Otherwise, it wouldn't make sense to call it an *object* of a certain *type*.

2. The object is pinned only for as long as a `pin_ptr` points to it. If a `pin_ptr` is reassigned or assigned `nullptr`, then the original object is no longer pinned. It is analogous to losing a reference to a managed object, thereby making it a candidate for GC.

3. The object being pinned can be either a value type or a member of a managed object, although not the object itself. If the managed object is an array, the pinning can be attempted only on its element while the entire array will be pinned.

4. A pin_ptr can only be a variable on the stack. In other words, during a GC, the only possible root for an object to skip compaction should be on the stack. This is to reduce the pinning scope of the object from being pinned forever. By limiting it to a local variable on the stack, it is implicit the variable will eventually fall out of scope, and the object will be unpinned.

Here is a quick example:

```cpp
using namespace System;
using namespace cli;

void SomeUnmanagedFunc(wchar_t* str, int length){
        for (int index = 0; index < size; ++index)
        {
                str[index] = towupper(str[index]);
        }
}

void SomeMixedModeFunc()
{
        cli::array<Char>^ chars = gcnew array<Char>(5) {
                'H', 'e', 'l', 'l', 'o'
        };

        pin_ptr<Char> pp = &chars[0];
        SomeUnmanagedFunc(pp, chars->Length);
        for(int index = 0; index < chars->Length; ++index)
        {
                Console::Write(chars[index]);
        }
}
```

In the preceding example, an unmanaged function SomeUnmanagedFunc is called to alter/update the contents of a managed array chars. Note, as already mentioned in pin_ptr rule number 3, although the first element of the array

(&chars[0]) is used for pinning, the entire array chars is pinned. Only an element of the array can be used for pinning.

interior_ptr<type>

C++/CLI code, whether purely managed or purely unmanaged or mixed mode, runs on the .NET CLR—meaning it is subject to garbage collection. The GC follows a contiguous mode allocation pattern for allocating memory. Compaction occurs (just like a disk defragmenter) whenever GC reclaims memory from garbage objects. Doing so changes the addresses of the objects that escaped the collection. But the GC updates the already existing live references to point to the newly moved locations. However, such an update does not happen on a native pointer that might be referring to reference types or its members.

To handle such a scenario, we require an entity that is not only pointer like, but it's superset. That means it must be able to point to a native or managed object, with a seamless syntax. It must allow all operations, arithmetic too, if it points to a native object. Enter interior_ptr.

- An interior_ptr can point to a member of a reference type, an element of a managed array, or any native object compatible with a native pointer.

- An interior pointer can only be declared on the stack. Therefore, it cannot be declared as a member of a class. They can be local variables or method parameters.

- A method with interior_ptr, instead of an equivalent native counterpart, has the advantage of a seamless syntax and works the same way.

The following is an example of using an `interior_ptr`:

```
ref class MgdClass
{
public: int dmNumber;
};

class UnmgdClass
{
public: int dmNumber;
};

void UserMethod()
{
  MgdClass^ objRef = gcnew MgdClass();
  interior_ptr<mgdclass^> ip1 = &objRef
  (*ip1)->dmNumber = 100;

  interior_ptr<int> ip2 = &(objRef->dmNumber);
  *ip2 = 200;

  // ip1 and ip2 are valid even after memory compaction.

  UnmgdClass *umObjRef = new UnmgdClass();
  interior_ptr<unmgdclass> ip3 = umObjRef;
  ip3->dmNumber = 500;

  interior_ptr<int> ip4 = &(umObjRef->dmNumber);
  *ip4 = 600;

  int num = 1000;
  interior_ptr<int> ip5 = &num;
  *ip5 = 200;
}
```

A method that takes an `interior_ptr` as a parameter instead of a raw pointer will have the flexibility to accept any of the `interior_ptrs` declared previously.

Generics

What templates mean to C++, so does generics to C++/CLI. But C++/CLI supports both templates and generics and allows mixing them too. Generics is a feature of the CLR, and C++\CLI has its own syntax (like C# and VB.NET) to make use of the feature.

Before delving into generics, let's think back a bit on templates. Unlike generics, templates is a *compile time only* feature. So each instantiation of the template creates a new runtime type based on the type parameters used. You could think of it as a syntactic way, although not just a syntactic sugar, to avoid code proliferation when it is possible to generalize the implementation. Once compiled to binary, the template classes/methods are no longer available or identified as they were declared in code. Each instantiation of the template creates a discrete type per type parameter(s) with mangled, compiler-generated, unique names.

Also note that if a C++ template class/method, although declared, is not instantiated anywhere in the code, it is omitted from the binary.

© Vivek Ragunathan 2016

V. Ragunathan, *C++/CLI Primer*, DOI 10.1007/978-1-4842-2367-3_23

Template classes and methods are not identified as declared in code at runtime; instead, they have compiler-generated names.

On the contrary, generics, apart from providing the facility of templates, are independent types themselves that are preserved even postcompilation. All instances of a particular generic type, say SomeClass<T>, are of the same generic type. All instances of SomeClass<T>, with T as int, are of the same type. This is an important distinction compared to templates.

It is only at runtime that the specialized type instance, say SomeClass<int>, is created. Until then, generic types (SomeClass<T>) exist in the assembly as one among several other types. That means that unlike templates, generic types are always part of the assembly even when they are not used/referred anywhere in the code. For instance, if SomeClass<T> was declared but not used anywhere in the code, it would still be part of the assembly; this is not so if it was a template.

Let's try to get a sense of the feature with a couple of examples:

Example—Generic Method

```
// Example - Generic Method
public ref class Utils
{
public: generic<typename U> static List<U>^ ToList
        (cli::array<U>^ arr)
{
        List<U>^ list = gcnew List<U>();

        for each (U item in arr)
        {
                list->Add(item);
        }

        return list;
}
};

// Usage snippet ...
cli::array<int>^ arr = gcnew array<int> { 1, 2, 3, 4, 5 };
List<int>^ list = Utils::ToList<int>(arr);
....
```

Example—Generic Class

```
using namespace System;
using namespace System::Collections::Generic;
using namespace System::Diagnostics;

generic<typename T> ref struct MyStack
{
private: List<T>^ stackElements;

public: MyStack(int minSize)
{
        this->stackElements = gcnew List<T>(minSize);
}

public: ~MyStack()
{
        Console::WriteLine("~MyStack()");
        this->stackElements->Clear();
}

public: !MyStack()
{
        Console::WriteLine("!MyStack()");
}

public: void Push(T item)
{
        Debug::Assert(item != nullptr, "Insert null items
                               not supported");
        stackElements->Add(item);
}

public: T Pop()
{
        T item = stackElements[stackElements->Count - 1];
        Debug::Assert(item != nullptr);
        stackElements->RemoveAt(stackElements->Count - 1);
        return item;
}
```

```
public: property int Size
{
        int get()
        {
                return this->stackElements->Count;
        }
}
};
```

The following is client code using the Stack<T> class:

```
// Sample code using the Stack<T> class on the heap and on
   the stack
void StackOnStackTest()
{
        Console::WriteLine("\nRunning StackOnStackTest ...");

        MyStack<int> stack(10);

        for (int index = 0; index < 10; ++index)
        {
                stack.Push(index + 1);
        }

        Console::WriteLine("Added {0} elements to the
        stack", stack.Size);

        while (stack.Size > 0)
        {
                const int value = stack.Pop();
                Console::WriteLine(
          "Popped {0} from the stack. Stack Size: {1}",
          value,
          stack.Size
        );
        }
}
```

```
void StackOnHeapTest()
{
        Console::WriteLine("\nRunning StackOnHeapTest ...");

        MyStack<int>^ stack = gcnew MyStack<int>(10);

        for (int index = 10; index < 20; ++index)
        {
                stack->Push(index + 1);
        }

        Console::WriteLine("Added {0} elements to the
        stack", stack->Size);

        while (stack->Size > 0)
        {
                const int value = stack->Pop();
                Console::WriteLine(
          "Popped {0} from the stack. Stack Size: {1}",
          value,
          stack->Size
        );

        }
}
```

Unlike C++ templates that are awaiting constraints, called **concepts**, for a long time now, C++/CLI generics has support for type constraints. That means you can restrict what kind of types are supported by a particular generic class/method.

```
generic <typename T> where T : IComparable<T>, gcnew
ref class SomeClass {
public: static String^ AsString(T instance)
        {
                return instance == T() ? "**NULL**" :
                                instance.ToString();
        }
}
```

The following are some observations that we make from the preceding example:

- SomeClass<T> will accept *only* types that implement the IComparable interface.

- Although generic-type parameters such as T previously can accept both managed and unmanaged types, we can restrict to only managed/ref types by specifying the gcnew constraint.

- T() is not creating an instance but denotes using the default value of T. Using nullptr directly in the method is not valid because T is not restricted to reference types. Value types cannot be null. If T needs to be constrained only to reference types, then where T : ref class should be used.

Unlike C#, C++/CLI allows enum to be specified in the type constraint.

What's more adventurous in C++/CLI is not generics and templates in silos but the mix. That's right! Templates and generics can coexist. Isn't it cool ? A template class can have generic classes and/or methods, but the other way around is not possible or allowed. Imagine why!

I'll give you a hint: templates need to be instantiated in code to make it into the assembly. Also, discrete types are created per instantiation per type parameter.

Here is an example of a managed template class:

```
template<typename T> ref class SomeClass
{
        public: void SomeMethod()
        {
                ...
        }
};
```

Although managed, the class follows the same template rules. That means one such managed type would be created per instantiation per type. Also, SomeClass can be specialized, such as the one following:

```
template<> ref class SomeClass<int>
{
        public: void SomeMethod()
        {
                ...
        }
};
```

Generics is a considerably vast area and requires devoting time for exploration and revelation. You can read more about generics at https://msdn.microsoft.com/en-us/library/8z2kbc1y.aspx.

The
Beginning

Well, there is only way to conclude. Let me put it this way. C++\CLI is not uglier but mightier and superior. The syntax might be a bit wild, and the concepts may be unconventional for a C++ programmer. But on the whole, the real power is unleashed by the capacity of the programmer. What you saw in this book has brought you only to the doors of power programming on the .NET platform. There is a lot more to explore and a lot of ways in which the language can be exploited for the better. It is only limited to our imagination.

I hope that the topics discussed in the book have kindled your interest to delve further and prove to be useful in your endeavors with C++/CLI.

For a lot more information on C++/CLI and the .NET, Microsoft Developer Network (at https://msdn.micro-soft.com/en-us/default.aspx) is one of the best places that I would recommend.

© Vivek Ragunathan 2016
V. Ragunathan, *C++/CLI Primer*, DOI 10.1007/978-1-4842-2367-3_24

Index

A

Abstract class
    C++/CLI class, 47
    description, 47
    explanatory code, 47
    virtual functions, 47

American National Standards
    Institute/International
    Organization for
    Standardization
    (ANSI/ISO), 4, 10

Application Program
    Interfaces (APIs), 5

Array
    BCL, 63
    cli:array class, 61
    integers, 62–63
    interior_ptr<type>, 69–70
    language-defined type, 61
    System::array type, 61

Assembly, 8

Automatic memory
    management, 21

B

Base Class Library (BCL), 7, 63

Boxing process, 27, 29

C

C++\CLI programming language,
    1, 3, 5, 9–11, 17, 20, 23,
    24, 38, 79

C++ destructor, 31, 36

Clone() method, 25

Common Type System (CTS), 9

C++ stack-based object
    semantics, 40

D

Directory instance, 25

dirObj variable, 40

Dispose method, 40

Dispose pattern
    implementation, 34

Dispose cleanup, 32–33

© Vivek Ragunathan 2016
V. Ragunathan, *C++/CLI Primer*, DOI 10.1007/978-1-4842-2367-3

Get the eBook for only $4.99!

Why limit yourself?

Now you can take the weightless companion with you wherever you go and access your content on your PC, phone, tablet, or reader.

Since you've purchased this print book, we are happy to offer you the eBook for just $4.99.

Convenient and fully searchable, the PDF version enables you to easily find and copy code—or perform examples by quickly toggling between instructions and applications.

To learn more, go to http://www.apress.com/us/shop/companion or contact support@apress.com.

Printed in the United States
By Bookmasters